ANCIENT CIVILIZATIONS

India

By Julie Nelson

Steadwell Books

Raintree Steck-Vaughn Publishers

A Harcourt Company

Austin · New York

www.steck-vaughn.com

Published by Raintree Steck-Vaughn Publishers, an imprint of Steck-Vaughn Company.

Library of Congress Cataloging-in-Publication Data
India/by Julie Nelson.
    p.cm.—(Ancient civilizations)
    Includes bibliographical references and index.
    ISBN 0-7398-3583-1
    1. India—Civilization—To 1200—Juvenile literature. [1. India—Civilization—To 1200.] I. Title. II. Ancient civilizations (Raintree Steck-Vaughn)
DS425 .N38 2001
934'21—dc21

                                                        2001019506

Printed and bound in the United States of America
1 2 3 4 5 6 7 8 9 10 WZ 05 04 03 02 01

Produced by Compass Books

Photo Acknowledgments
Unicorn Stock Photos, Jean Higgins, cover;
Corbis/Brian Vikander,12; Hans Georg Roth, 19; Lindsay Hebberd, 30;
    Charles and Josette Lenars, 34; Hulton-Deutsch Collection, 36
J.M. Kenoyer, 6, 9, 22, 25, 40
Photo Network/Mark Newman, 10; Stephen Saks, 20
Root Resources/Byron Crader, 32; Sang H. Kriek, 43
Visuals Unlimited/Charles Philip, title page; T.J. Malhotra, 16;
    Joe McDonald, 26, 29

Content Consultants
John Adams
Sawhill Associates

Don L. Curry
Educational Author, Editor, Consultant, and Columnist

Contents

History of Ancient India

India has one of the world's oldest and longest-lasting civilizations. In a civilization, people are part of an **advanced society** and share a way of life. Civilization in India has lasted for more than 5,000 years.

Indian civilization has lasted so long partly because the country is difficult for enemies to attack by land or sea. The Himalayan Mountains separate India from other countries to the north. In the south, the ocean surrounds the country on three sides.

The Vindhya Mountains and the Namada River divide northern and southern India. Different civilizations formed in the north and the south.

▲ This illustration shows what the buildings looked like in Harappa.

The Indus Valley Civilization

In about 2,500 B.C., Dravidian people started the Indus Civilization. This was the first known civilization in India. It started in the Indus Valley, which surrounds the Indus River in northwestern India. The river provided the Dravidians with water, fish, and a way to move goods from one place to another. Indian people began building large, well-planned cities along the river. There were more than 1,400 Indus cities. Two of the main cities were Harappa and Mohenjo-Daro. About 35,000 people lived in each city.

All large cities were planned and built the same way. A 30-foot (9-m) wide street traveled north to south through the city. Other streets traveled east to west, crossing the main street. Sewers were under the streets. Waste from people's houses flowed through clay pipes into the sewers and out of the city. A citadel rose from the center of the city. A citadel is a military fort. A tall wall with towers surrounded the citadel. Soldiers kept watch from the towers. Some cities also had a large pool for bathing.

People lived in brick houses with one or two levels. The rooms were built around an open area called a courtyard. Windows looked out into the courtyard. Houses often had their own wells and pools for bathing. Many also had bathrooms.

Farming

Farming was the center of Indus life. Land in the Indus Valley was good for growing crops. Dravidians used wooden plows to break up the soil. Then they planted seeds. They grew cotton, fruit, vegetables, and grains, such as barley and wheat.

Each town had a granary, or a place to store grain. People brought their crops to the granary. Everyone shared the food throughout the year.

Writing

The Indus people used **pictograph** writing. Pictographs are pictures and symbols that stand for words and objects. There were about 500 different pictographs.

Archaeologists have not been able to figure out how to read the Dravidian language. Archaeologists are scientists who study the past.

▲ This is a sample of pictograph writing from ancient Harappa.

What Happened?

After about 800 years, the Indus Valley Civilization slowly came to an end. By 1,750 B.C., people had left the cities and towns. Archaeologists are not sure what happened. They think maybe the river flooded, or the soil became too poor for growing crops. Some archaeologists think other groups attacked the Dravidians.

▲ These are the remains of a Hindu temple.
Hinduism started during the Epic Period.

The Vedic and Epic Periods

Beginning in 1,749 B.C., Aryan people
moved to India from Central Asia. They
belonged to clans. A clan is a group of
people with common relatives. A warrior
chief ruled each clan.

Aryans spoke a language called Sanskrit.
They also practiced their own religion. **Priests**

made offerings and said prayers to the gods. Priests are people who serve the gods.

The Aryans wrote about their beliefs and customs in the Rig-Veda. A **Veda** is a book of religious songs and poems. The period of Indian civilization between 1,749 to 1,000 B.C. became known as the Vedic Period.

Between 1,000 and 323 B.C., important Indian epics were written. An epic is a poem about a hero or god. This period in history became known as the Epic Period.

People's way of life changed during the Epic Period. Some people began practicing the religion of Hinduism. A king ruled over large areas. He collected taxes from people.

Also during this time, the Aryans first divided people into groups. This was called the **caste** system. Each caste was called a jati. Jatis were grouped into levels called varnas. People belonged to a varna based on the job they did. For example, there were potter jatis, shoemaker jatis, and cloth-making jatis.

▲ These remains are temples and pillars that were built while Ashoka was king.

The Mauryans

In 322 B.C., King Chandragupta Maurya became the first Mauryan king. Mauryan kings ruled India from 322 to 185 B.C. The Mauryans set up India's first central government. King Chandragupta Maurya united northern India and some of southern

India into one large empire. Empires are made of many kingdoms ruled by one king.

The king divided the empire into parts called provinces. A governor or a prince was in charge of each province. Each province was divided into districts run by deputies. Each district was then divided into villages. A chief and a council of helpers ran each village. The Mauryan kings collected taxes from the people. They used the taxes to pay for an army, to feed the poor, and to build hospitals and roads. The Mauryans also built rest houses for travelers next to the roads.

Ashoka was a famous Mauryan king. He was the first Indian king to create a set of laws. Laws are the rules people must follow. Ashoka had workers carve the laws and other sayings onto rocks and pillars. A pillar is a tall, round column. He placed the rocks and pillars throughout his empire for people to read. Today, you can still see some of Ashoka's columns.

The Guptas

After Ashoka died, weak Mauryan kings could not keep the empire together. Kingdoms began ruling themselves again. In 185 B.C., the rule of the last Mauryan king ended. From 185 B.C. to A.D. 320, different groups fought each other for power. Satavahana kings ruled northern India. Kushana kings ruled southern India.

Gupta kings ruled from A.D. 320 to 520. They formed most of northern India into a large empire. Like the Mauryans, the Guptas set up a central government and collected taxes. They also had a large army.

Gupta kings supported Hinduism. But Indians had religious freedom. They could practice their own religions.

Some archaeologists call the Gupta Period the Golden or the Classical Age of India. During this period, people created buildings, art, and music. They also made important scientific discoveries.

INDIA TIMELINE

2500 B.C. to 1750 B.C.	Indus Valley Civilization rules Indus Valley area.
1749 B.C. to 323 B.C..	India goes through changes in the Vedic and Epic Periods.
322 B.C. to 185 B.C.	Powerful kings control India during the Mauryan Period.
185 B.C. to A.D. 320	Satavahana kings rule southern India, while Kushana kings rule northern India.
A.D. 320 to A.D. 520	During this Golden Age of India, Gupta kings rule large parts of the country.

Around A.D. 453 the Huns began attacking the Gupta empire. The Guptas were able to protect their empire for awhile. But by A.D. 500, the Huns had become too powerful. They took over much of the Gupta's land. The Gupta empire had ended by A.D. 520.

Indians from higher varnas wore expensive gold jewelry.

Daily Life in Ancient India

Ancient Indian Hindu society was divided into the caste system. There were four different **social** levels, or varnas. Children were born into the varna of their parents.

Brahmans were members of the first varna, the **brahma**. Brahmans were priests or teachers.

Rulers and warriors were members of the second varna, or the **kshatriya**.

The third varna was the **vaisya**. Merchants and craftspeople were members of the vaisya. Merchants bought, sold, or traded goods.

The fourth varna was the **sudra**. Workers belonged to the sudra. They farmed, raised animals, and worked for other people.

Learning in Ancient India

Not all children in ancient India went to school. Boys and girls were treated differently. Children in different varnas received different lessons.

Boys started learning at home. They learned the alphabet at four or five years of age. Reading and basic math were taught by a tutor or a teacher in a village or local school. Teachers taught classes outdoors. At recess students learned sports.

After basic education, boys from lower varnas learned job skills from their fathers. Then they worked.

Boys from the three highest varnas went beyond basic education. They went away to live in community schools with a **guru**, or a teacher. These schools were called hermitages or ashrams. They were simple shacks that were often in the forest. Students did all the work. They washed the school and their clothes, and they cooked. They also begged for their food.

These are the ruins of an ancient Indian ashram where boys studied.

Girls were not always given as much education as boys. Some were tutored at home. Others attended ashrams or learned to become dancers or actors. Girls learned how to run a household from their mothers.

Indians sometimes wore turbans like this to protect their heads from the Sun.

Indian Clothing

The basic dress of ancient India was a long piece of cloth wrapped around the body many times. In colder weather, people wore more cloth. Cotton and wool were the most popular cloths. Rich Indians began wearing silk in 1 B.C. Silk is cloth made from the cocoons of silkworms.

Men in ancient India wore a **dhoti**. A dhoti was a piece of cloth around 30 feet (9 m) long. It wrapped around the legs and was tied at the waist. It looked like baggy pants. If it was very hot, men just wore a loincloth. This long strip of cloth wrapped around the waist, pulled through the legs, and tied in front.

Women in ancient India wore a brightly colored **sari**. This long piece of cloth wrapped around the body and draped over the shoulder. Sometimes women wore a dhoti with a tight, backless blouse called a **choli**.

At times, both men and women wore turbans. A turban is a piece of cloth wrapped around the head.

Some people in higher varnas wore jewelry. This included rings for the ears, nose, fingers, and toes. Rich people also wore bands on their arms and ankles. Women wrapped gold and silver chains around their waists and in their hair.

These are the remains of an ancient Indian house.

Indian Houses

People in higher varnas had larger houses than people in lower varnas. Village houses were smaller than houses in large cities.

Village houses were one level high and made of straw, bamboo, or wood. Most of these houses had only one to two square or round rooms. People covered the outer walls with mud to keep out the cold or heat. The floors were made of dirt. The roof was made of palm leaves or reeds. Most people had a bed made of bamboo or wood and maybe a table. They usually sat on floor rugs when they ate.

Rich people in cities had houses made of brick or wood. The houses were several levels high. A staircase connected the levels. The houses were rectangle-shaped and built around a courtyard. The houses often had gardens and pools behind them. A balcony on the upper level of the home overlooked the gardens.

Tapestries hung from ceilings and divided the rooms. A tapestry is a piece of cloth that has pictures or designs on it. The floors were made of tiles and covered with carpet. At night people lit their homes with oil-burning lamps.

Indian Meals

Rice was the basic food of Indians in ancient times. It was cooked and served with every meal. In the northwest, wheat was made into flour. Another common food was lentils. A lentil is a kind of dried bean. A favorite meal was **curry**, a rice dish with a spicy gravy. A popular snack food was capati, a kind of pancake. Other dishes were fruit, vegetables, or meat. Many Indians did not eat meat because of their religious beliefs.

People from higher varnas ate many sweet desserts. Honey was used on special occasions. Most people drank either milk or water with their meals.

Ancient Indian cooking was known for its spices. Spices included cinnamon, salt, pepper, ginger, basil, and cloves.

Indians followed careful rituals when eating meals. A ritual is a way of doing things in order. The father of the house ate before everyone else. His children washed his

People in higher varnas ate on plates like this one.

feet before the meal. The mother followed in the same way. The children ate last.

Often people in lower varnas used banana leaves for dishes. They threw the leaves away when they were finished eating. People in higher varnas ate from pottery. Pottery is objects made of clay, such as plates, cups, and bowls.

This carving of a Hindu god decorated the outside of a temple.

Ancient Indian Culture

T he **culture** of a group of people is their way of life, ideas, and traditions. The Indians expressed their culture in the things they made. Ancient India's culture was tied very closely to their religion. Everything the people did was guided by their religious beliefs.

Most people of ancient India were Hindus. This means they followed the religion of Hinduism. There are many different gods and goddesses in Hinduism.

Some people in ancient India followed Buddhism. This religion is based on the teachings of Siddhartha, who is also called Buddha. Artists made many different carvings and statues of Buddha and events from his life.

Art

The purpose of most ancient Indian art was to honor the gods. There were many carvings of Buddha and of Hindu gods and goddesses. These works of art were often found on **temple** walls. Large statues of Buddha and the gods sat in the temples. The statues showed worshipers the power of the gods.

Art also showed Indians' love of nature. Common images in carvings and pictures were animals, plants, and flowers.

Some kings hired artists to create pieces of art. These pieces of art often showed kings battling India's enemies. The purpose of this art was to show the wealth and power of kings.

Indian artists were well-known for the style of their statues and carvings. A style is a look and way of making something. Statues were simple, not detailed. They did not look like real people.

Small works of art were common as well. These included small clay statues of gods and

goddesses in palaces and people's homes. Clay plaques showed scenes from people's daily lives. A plaque is a plate with words or pictures on it, usually placed on a wall. Artists also made toys, such as whistles and dolls.

This modern dancer is performing an ancient Indian dance.

Literature

Ancient Indians of the higher varnas spoke and wrote in a common language called Sanskrit. All the holy Hindu books were written in Sanskrit. This language had many rules. People had to study the language for many years to read and write it well.

Indian writers wrote to teach people about the gods. They also tried to stir feelings in their readers. Indians believed there were nine main feelings: love, happiness, anger, sadness, courage, fear, hate, wonder, and peace. Writers tried to include a balance of these feelings in their stories.

Dancers performed plays and other works of literature. Like writers, dancers tried to stir the feelings of the people watching. In the Gupta period, there were 13 ways to hold the head, 36 eye movements, 37 hand movements, nine ways to move the neck, and 10 ways to hold the body. Each movement meant something different. It took years for dancers to learn these special dance moves.

Indian temples were decorated with many
different carvings of the gods.

Indian Architecture

Architecture is a style of building. Indians
in ancient times expressed themselves by
building temples. The style of building
depended on the current leader's religion
and beliefs. Kings ordered great buildings to

be built. They used taxes to pay workers who helped build temples, hospitals, and other public buildings.

Indian temples were known for their decorations. Almost every part was either carved or covered with paintings.

Hindu temples were square and built on a raised platform. Steps led up the platform to the main temple. Temples usually had one or more towers in the middle. The buildings were made of stone so they would last a long time. Pillars often decorated the front of the temples.

A special kind of Buddhist temple was called a stupa. A stupa was a round dome made of brick or stone. A carved stone railing surrounded the stupa. Large temples often had smaller stupas surrounding one large stupa. Stupas sometimes held the remains of famous Buddhist leaders. Stupas were also built in important places from Buddha's life.

This is a picture of a Gupta prince. Gupta rulers built many hospitals and temples.

What Did the Ancient Indians Do?

Ancient Indian scientists made many important discoveries. Some of their most important work was in the field of medicine. In the Mauryan and Gupta Periods, kings had hospitals built. Poor people received free medical care. Many doctors studied new ways to treat sicknesses.

One well-known Indian doctor was Sushruta. He wrote a medical book in the fourth century. The book told doctors how to make medicines from different plants. It also explained that people should be clean and should exercise to stay healthy.

 Indian scientists studied the stars at this ancient observatory.

Astronomy

Ancient Indian astronomers studied at observatories. An astronomer is a scientist who studies objects in space. An observatory is a place where people watch objects in the sky. Astronomers studied the position of the

Did you know that the Indian writer Kalidasa is often called the Indian Shakespeare? Kalidasa lived during the Gupta Period. He wrote famous plays and poems about gods and kings. People still read his stories today.

planets, the Sun, the Moon, and the stars. They tracked the movements of these objects across the sky. They used the placement of the stars to predict events. To predict is to guess what will happen in the future.

One famous astronomer was Aryabhata. In the fifth century, he made some important discoveries. He learned that Earth was round. Most people of his time thought that the Sun and stars orbit Earth. To orbit is to go around in a set path. Aryabhata said that Earth orbits the Sun. Also, he discovered that Earth spins around its axis. An axis is an imaginary line through the center of a round object like a planet or baseball. Aryabhata's image of a round, spinning Earth orbiting the Sun has turned out to be correct.

Math

Indian mathematicians changed the way the world's people use numbers. A mathematician is a scientist who studies mathematics or math. They learned how to use the numbers zero through nine to make all the large numbers. The new numbers made it possible to show different place notations for tens, hundreds, and thousands. They could take a 2 and a 7 and make them stand for 27 or 227 or 7,222. These are the numbers we still use today.

Indian scientists also did problems with negative numbers. They understood that if you had a +4 and a -4, you got 0, or zero, when you added them together. Indian mathematicians were the first to make zero, or nothing, a useful number.

Because of the place notations and the zero, people could easily do division and multiplication problems.

The Decimal System

10 x	.1 =	1
10 x	1 =	10
10 x	10 =	100
10 x	100 =	1,000
10 x	1,000 =	10,000
10 x	10,000 =	100,000
10 x	100,000 =	1,000,000

This chart shows how the decimal system works.

The new numbers made the decimal system possible. The Indian math system was based on the number ten and is used around the world today.

Archaeologists study ruins of ancient Indian cities like this one.

How Do We Know?

Archaeology helps us understand ancient India. Archaeology is the study of the past. There are many ways to understand the culture of ancient India using archaeology. By studying the art of that time, we know what people wore and ate. We can see what animals they hunted and who their kings, gods, and heroes were.

Archaeologists also study the ruins of ancient cities. They can see how cities were built, what buildings were like, and how people lived. They also examine **artifacts**. Artifacts are objects made or used by humans in the past, such as dishes and tools.

Ajanta Caves

In 1819, a group of British hunters discovered the Ajanta caves. During the Gupta Period, Indian workers carved these caves into a U-shaped rock cliff. It took workers more than 20 years to make the caves.

There are 29 caves at Ajanta. Some of the caves are carved more than 100 feet (30 m) into the cliff. A huge statue of Buddha sits outside the caves. Large pillars and carved stone surround the entrance. Inside, the ceilings and walls are covered with colorful murals, or wall-sized paintings. Artists carved scenes from Buddha's life on some cave walls. Other pictures are of daily life. Archaeologists think that a few of the caves were Buddhist temples. Other rooms in the caves were probably rooms where priests lived.

Ancient India Ideas Today

The culture of ancient India is still important today. Students in India still learn the Vedas. Modern Indian dancers practice the

 Many people visit the Ajanta caves each year.

moves of the ancient dancers. The flag of India has the symbol of King Ashoka in its center.

Hinduism and Buddhism are important world religions. Many people practice Hinduism or follow the teachings of Buddha.

People around the world are interested in the belief system and ideas of ancient India. Each year, millions of people travel to India to see temples and ruins.

advanced (ad-VANST)—highly developed

ancient (AYN-shunt)—very old

archaeology (ar-kee-OL-uh-jee)—study of the past of humankind

architecture (AR-kuh-tek-chur)—style of building

artifact (ART-uh-fakt)—object made and used by humans in the past

brahma (BRAH-muh)—highest varna, made up of priests and scholars

caste (KAST)—a system of grouping people based on their jobs

choli (CHOL-ee)—tight-fitting blouse

culture (KUHL-chur)—way of life and customs of a group of people

curry (KUR-ee)—rice dish served with a spicy gravy

dhoti (DOH-tee)—clothing made of fabric tied around the legs and waist

guru (goo-ROO)—teacher

kshatriya (KSHAT-ree-ah)—second highest varna, made up of soldiers and rulers

pictograph (PIK-toh-graf)—a picture used as a symbol for a word or sound

priest (PREEST)—men who served the gods and worked in temples

sari (SAR-ee)—clothing made of fabric wrapped around the body like a dress

social (SOH-shuhl)—having to do with the way that people live together as a society

society (suh-SYE-uh-tee)—all the people who live in the same area and share the same customs and laws

sudra (SOO-drah)—fourth varna, made up of workers

temple (TEM-puhl)—a special building used for worshiping gods

vaisya (VIS-yah)—third varna, made up of traders and merchants

Veda (VAY-duh)—ancient Hindu book of knowledge

Internet Sites

Ancient India
http://www.penncharter.com/Student/india/
index.html

Daily Life in Ancient India
http://members.aol.com/Donnclass/Indialife.
html

Discover India
http://www.india-web.com/history.htm

Electronic Passport to India
http://www.mrdowling.com/612india.html

Indolink: Kidz Korner
http://www.indolink.com/Kidz/main.html

Useful Addresses

The Government of India Tourist Office
1270 Avenue of Americas
Suite 1808
New York, NY 10020

Indian Museum-Calcutta
27 Jawarharlal Nehru Road
Calcutta 700013
India

Museum of Archaeology and Ethnology
Department of Archaeology
Simon Fraser University
8888 University Drive
Burnaby, BC V5A 1S6
Canada

Index